# HOMEMADE
# SOAP MAKING

## Project Book

Learn how to make a collection
of homemade soaps

10 projects inside

# INTRODUCTION

The art of homemade soap is a great way to get creative and learn new skills. These tempting bathroom treats won't fail to deliver and they always smell so good! Wrapped with a piece of string, your DIY soaps make the most beautiful homemade gifts.

The best part of soap making is you get to pick exactly what goes into them! By including natural ingredients and essential oils you can produce soaps which are better for your skin and for the planet.

In this kit we have provided everything you need for your beginner project which will get you started on your soap making journey. There are a number of further recipes to practice your skills and to help you find your perfect show stopping soap.

All our recipes in this book use the melt and pour method for our soap making.

Remember it can take time to master the process, so don't be discouraged if your soap isn't perfect on the first attempt. You just need to keep practising and experimenting and you will get there in no time.

Let's get started!

# KIT CONTENTS

## WHAT'S INCLUDED:

Soap base mixture
Soap mould
Stirring rod
Pipette
Dried rose petals

## WHAT YOU'LL NEED:

Cooker hob or microwave for melting
the soap base
Heatproof bowl
Saucepan
Water
Rose essential oil (optional)
Thermometer (optional)

If you want a more professional finish
then you can also use rubbing alcohol
in a spray bottle on the soap. This is
optional and helps to give the soap a
completely smooth finish.

# MELTING YOUR SOAP:

The easiest way to melt your soap is to use the double boiler method. Take your saucepan and add approximately 2 inches of water, slowly bring to the boil.

Whilst the water is simmering, place a heatproof glass bowl on top of the pan and add your soap mixture, stirring until it has fully melted.

# TEMPERATURE:

Temperature is key when using the melt and pour process. The ideal range is between 48C and 54C (although you should check with specific manufacturers regarding their ranges).

# ALCOHOL SPRAY:

Rubbing alcohol is useful for any soap maker. This can help achieve a professional finish on your soaps. Spraying your soap with alcohol helps to remove any surface bubbles.

It's also a good way to stick additional components like flowers or seeds to your finished soaps.

# INGREDIENTS:

Choosing the right herbs and flowers is a key part of soap making. There are so many wonderful options to choose from. They not only help to add colour but also fragrance and decoration to your soaps. There are also lots of benefits for your skin and body so be sure to read up on your ingredients and their benefits befor using them.

Some of our favourite ingredients are rosemary, peppermint, lavender, lemon balm, chamomile, rose oil, orange and grapefruit!

When you are new to soap making it can be a little overwhelming at first. Start by getting the basics right and then you can work on perfecting your craft.

It is best to practice your soap making, you can experiment with different techniques until you get a way that works best for you. Our starter project should help you to learn the basic technique of melt and pour. You can then move onto the other projects in this book to practice further.

# TIPS & TECHNIQUES:

Preparation is key when it comes to soap making. Always have all your ingredients and equipment ready before you start.

Sometimes your melt and pour can start to solidify before you're ready to pour. Don't worry if this happens, you can always put the mix back into the bowl and re-melt.

Flowers are a great way to decorate your soap, they look beautiful. However it is best to only add them onto the top of your soap when just set. The melt and pour mixture is water-based so it will cause dried flowers to turn brown after time. This is not a problem with the soap but it doesn't look too attractive so it's best to keep them on top of your soap only.

We always recommend using the soap within the first couple of weeks after making, it's always most fragrant then.

If your soap has fingerprints and marks from where you've handled it, you can simply spray some alcohol on it to remove any prints.

One of the best things about making your own soaps is the variety of shapes you can make. Household items such as wooden containers, plastic or even cookie cutters can all be lined with clingfilm ready for your soap mixture.

# WARNINGS!

All the makes included in this book are designed for adults and are not suitable for children under the age of 14. Always keep all ingredients and finished products out of the reach of children.

Some ingredients may irritate; always avoid contact with skin and eyes. If ingredients come into contact with eyes or skin, wash with cold water immediately for five minutes minimum.

Do not ingest; if accidentally ingested drink water and seek medical advice.

Due to some of the ingredients in the soap bases – always wear gloves when handling.

We recommend wearing old clothes or overalls when partaking in creative activities. Cover work surfaces to avoid mess.

**MAKES
1**

**15 MINS
TO MAKE**

MAKE
WITH KIT
CONTENTS!

# ROSE
# PETAL

10

# ROSE PETAL

These rose petal soaps are easy to make and are perfect to enjoy yourself or give to a loved one. The ingredients for this project are included in your kit and have been pre-measured for you.

## YOU WILL NEED

- Heatproof bowl
- Heat resistant jug
- Saucepan
- Wooden spoon
- Thermometer (optional)
- Rose oil (optional)
- Rubbing alcohol in spray bottle (optional)

## KIT CONTENTS

- Soap mixture
- A rectangular silicone mould for your soap
- Rose petals

# METHOD

**1.** FIrst, get all of your kit contents and equipment ready. Make sure you set up your work surface close to your heating appliance, we would recommend setting up in the kitchen as you will be using a cooker hob.

**2.** Open up your soap base and leave to one side. At this point, place your mould onto a piece of old newspaper so it is ready for pouring into.

**3.** Take your rose petals and tear into smaller pieces, also leave some petals whole. Put these in a bowl and set aside for later.

**4.** As mentioned in the tips and tricks section, we recommend using the double boiler method to melt your soap. Add two inches of water to your saucepan and slowly bring to the boil. Whilst this is simmering, pour your soap mixture into the heatproof bowl and place on top of the saucepan.

**5.** Continue to stir the mixture and it should begin to melt.

**6.** If you have a thermometer you can use this to check the temperature, you are looking for around 48-54C. Alternatively, keep stirring until the mixture is fully melted.

**7.** Once fully melted, remove from the heat, be careful as it will be very hot.

**8.** Place the heated soap mix bowl onto a heat resistant mat or counter. CAUTION: The bowl will be very hot so handle carefully using a tea towel or oven gloves.

**9.** To get better pouring control into your mould, it is best to carefully transfer the mix into a heatproof glass jug. Slowly pour the melted mix from the bowl into a glass jug.

**10.** Pour the mixture into the mould until it nearly reaches the brim.

**11.** If you have alcohol spray available, spray the surface of your soap 4 – 5 times. This will pop any bubbles and a hard skin will start to form, leaving your soap smooth and wrinkle free.

**12.** The mixture will start to cool quite quickly, so you can begin to decorate straight away.

**13.** Get the petals you prepared earlier. Carefully place each of the full petal pieces onto the the soap first. Then you can sprinkle the smaller pieces over the top of these. Do this until you're happy with the finished look.

**14.** Leave the soap to set. You can put the soap in the fridge or freezer to speed up the process of setting, however a single mould like this should set within around 30 minutes.

**15.** Once fully set, carefully remove the soap from the mould and place onto a flat surface. That's it you're done!

**CAUTION:**

**The bowl will be very hot so handle carefully using a tea towel or oven gloves.**

**MAKES
6**

**15 MINS
TO MAKE**

# CITRUS
# ORANGE

# CITRUS ORANGE

This citrus orange soap is zesty and uplifting. The bright colour is like a ray of sunshine and will take you back to a warm summers day. As well as the fresh citrus smell, the dried orange makes this an irresistible present or bathroom showstopper.

## YOU WILL NEED

- Heatproof bowl
- Heatproof jug
- Saucepan
- Wooden spoon
- Measuring scales
- Rubbing alcohol spray
- Thermometer (optional)

## INGREDIENTS

- 455g aloe vera melt & pour base
- 6 cavity rectangular silicone mould
- Dried oranges
- Orange essential oil

# METHOD

**1.** Set up your work surface close to your heating appliance, as you did in the first project. Prepare your mould by spraying it with alcohol spray.

**2.** Take your melt and pour soap base and weigh out 455g.

**3.** You then need to cut the 455g of soap base into small cube size pieces, this will help it to melt quicker. Put this to one side until you are ready to melt.

**4.** Melt the soap base using the double boiler method as you did in the first project.

**5.** Once the soap has reached the correct temperature or fully melted, add the orange essential oil. We recommend using around 10 drops of oil. Once this is added, stir through until fully mixed into your melted soap base.

**6.** Take the melted soap off of the heat and place onto a heat resistant mat or heatproof counter.

**7.** To get better pouring control, we recommend you transfer the mix into a heatproof glass jug at this stage. CAUTION: The bowl will be very hot so handle carefully using a tea towel or oven gloves.

**8.** It's now time to pour the mixture into your mould, carefully pour it evenly into the six cavities. It is best to add a smaller amount to each cavity then gradually add a bit more until all six are filled to the same height. This will make sure they are a matching size and shape but make sure you act quickly as the soaps will start to set.

**9.** Remember to have your alcohol spray to hand and give each bar a good spritz after pouring to remove any bubbles on top. Always do this quickly before the soap begins to set.

**10.** To decorate your soaps, add a selection of dried orange pieces, carefully placing them on top of each soap mix in the mould. Try a mix of whole and half orange pieces and see what you prefer!

**11.** Leave your soaps to set.

**12.** Once fully set, carefully remove them from your mould and place onto a flat surface. If you are not planning on using your soaps straight away then tightly wrap them in clingfilm and unwrap when ready to use.

**TIP**
Tie the finished soaps with twine for the perfect homemade gift

**MAKES 6**

**15 MINS TO MAKE**

# LAVENDER

# LAVENDER

Create a relaxing and spa like scent with these lavender soap bars. The ideal soap for use before bed, the moisturising shea butter and calming lavender is the perfect combination.

## YOU WILL NEED

- Heatproof bowl
- Heatproof jug
- Saucepan
- Wooden spoon
- Measuring scales
- Rubbing alcohol spray
- Thermometer (optional)

## INGREDIENTS

- 455g shea butter melt and pour base
- 15g dried lavender
- 6 cavity rectangular silicone mould
- Lavender essential oil
- Fresh lavender (optional for decoration)

# METHOD

**1.** Set up your work surface and prepare your melt and pour soap base. Do this by weighing 455g of the base. You then need to cut the 455g of soap base into smaller pieces, this will help it to melt quicker.

**2.** Next prepare your mould by spraying it with alcohol spray. Then sprinkle some dried lavender into the bottom of each cavity of the mould.

**3.** Next you need to melt the soap base, use the double boiler method as you did in the first project.

**4.** Once the soap has melted, you can add in your essential oil. We recommend using 10 drops of lavender oil to the mix. Add a little more if you want a stronger scent. Once added, make sure you stir well until fully mixed into the melted mixture.

**5.** Next take off the heat and transfer the mix into a heatproof glass jug. Be careful when pouring as the bowl and mixture will be very hot.

**6.** It's now time to pour the mixture into your mould. Slowly pour into each cavity (making sure you distribute evenly). Remember to have your alcohol spray to hand and give each bar a good spritz after pouring to remove any bubbles on top. Always do this quickly before the soaps begin to set.

**7.** When you pour the mixture into the mould the lavender may start to rise. If you would like it to be mixed through your soap bars, then we suggest you stir each soap in the mould with a toothpick.

**8.** Leave your soaps to set, following the same process from the first project. Why not add a sprig of lavender with some string and a brown tag to make a lovely homemade gift!

**MAKES
12**

**60 MINS
TO MAKE**

# COFFEE

# COFFEE

One for coffee lovers. The deep coffee aroma is the perfect pick me up in the morning.

## YOU WILL NEED

- Heatproof bowl
- Heatproof jug
- Saucepan
- Wooden spoon
- Measuring scales
- Rubbing alcohol spray
- Thermometer (optional)
- Wire soap cutter or large knife to cut the soap loaf

## INGREDIENTS

- 1kg goats milk melt and pour base
- Instant coffee
- Vanilla essential oil
- 2lb loaf tin mould (lined with cling flim)
- Coffee beans (optional for decorating)

# METHOD

**1.** Set up your work surface and separate your soap mixture into 800g and 200g, and then cut each into small squares.

**2.** Next you should prepare your loaf tin mould, you will need to line the tin with cling film, ready to pour the soap into later. The cling film will help you to remove the soap when set. Also spray the lined tin with alchol spray to stop bubbles forming in your soap.

**3.** Take your 800g soap base and use the double boiler method as you did in the first project. This time, add 4 tablespoons of instant coffee to the melted mixture and stir through.

**4.** You should now add in your vanilla essential oil, we recommend 10 drops. Stir well.

**5.** Once the soap has reached the correct temperature or is fully melted, remove from the heat and place on a heat resistant mat. CAUTION: The bowl will be very hot so handle carefully using a tea towel or oven gloves. To get better pouring control, transfer the mix into a heatproof glass jug, as we did in the "rose petal" project.

**6.** It's now time to pour the mixture into your lined loaf tin mould and quickly spray the soap mix with alcohol spray.

**7.** Whilst this sets in the mould, take the remaining 200g and melt using the double boiler method. Add 6 tablespoons of instant coffee to the melted soap and stir well. This will create the darker top layer of the soap.

**8.** Once finished pour over your other mixture (this should have hardened in the mould now). Quickly spray again with alcohol spray as soon as you pour into the mould. You can decorate your soap with coffee beans on top if you want that extra special finish!

**9.** Leave your soap to set overnight in a cool, dry place. When completely set, remove from the mould and carefully cut into slices, we suggest between half an inch to 1 inch.

**TIP**

Using a wire soap cutter or loaf soap cutter will help you to cut the soaps into equal sizes.

**MAKES
6**

**15 MINS
TO MAKE**

# HONEY
# & OATS

# HONEY & OATS

A fun way to turn a breakfast classic into your new favourite soap. The honey gives a subtle sweet undertone, whilst also being known for it's natural benefits against oily skin. The oatmeal is a great exfoliator, meaning this offers a number of benefits, all in a natural soap bar.

## YOU WILL NEED

- Heatproof bowl
- Heatproof jug
- Saucepan
- Wooden spoon
- Measuring scales
- Rubbing alcohol spray
- Thermometer (optional)

## INGREDIENTS

- 455g shea butter melt and pour base
- 6 cavity rectangular silicone mould
- 2 tbsp honey
- 2 tbsp rolled oats
- Extra oats for decoration
- Vanilla essential oil

# METHOD

**1.** Set up your work surface and prepare your melt and pour soap base. Do this by weighing 455g of the base. You then need to cut the 455g of soap base into smaller pieces, this will help it to melt quicker.

**2.** Next prepare your mould by spraying it with alcohol spray.

**3.** Now you need to melt the soap base, use the double boiler method as you did in the first project.

**4.** Once the soap is melted, add in your oats, honey and essential oil. We recommend using 10 drops of vanilla oil to the mix. Add a little more if you want a stronger scent. Once added, make sure you stir well until all ingredients are fully mixed into the melted mixture.

**5.** Next take your bowl off the heat and transfer the mix into a heatproof glass jug. Be careful when pouring as the bowl and mixture will be very hot.

**6.** It's now time to pour the mixture into your mould. Slowly pour into each cavity (making sure you distribute evenly). Remember to have your alcohol spray to hand and give each bar a good spritz after pouring to remove any bubbles on top. Always do this quickly before the soaps begin to set.

**7.** Leave your soaps to set, following the same process from the first project.

Optional: you can add extra rolled oats to the top of your soaps as more decoration. Add as many as you like to create your own desired look.

**8.** When fully set, remove each soap from it's mould. You can use straight away or store with some cling film ready to use later!

**MAKES
12**

**30 MINS
TO MAKE**

# COCOA

# COCOA

Everyone's favourite treat ... chocolate. Cocoa actually helps renew skin cells, meaning you can have chocolate every day, without any of the guilt.

## YOU WILL NEED

- Heatproof bowl
- Heatproof jug
- Saucepan
- Wooden spoon
- Measuring scales
- Rubbing alcohol spray
- Thermometer (optional)
- Wire soap cutter to cut the soap loaf

## INGREDIENTS

- 1kg crystal melt and pour base
- 4 tbsp cocoa powder
- 125g dark chocolate (85% cocoa)
- Cocoa essential oil
- 2lb loaf tin mould
- Optional; Chocolate shavings for decoration

# METHOD

**1.** Set up your work surface and prepare your melt and pour soap base. Do this by weighing the base. You then need to cut the soap base into smaller cube pieces, this will help it to melt quicker.

**2.** Next prepare your loaf tin by lining it with cling film and then spraying it with alcohol spray.

**3.** Prepare the cocoa powder by putting around 3 tablespoons of cocoa powder into a bowl. Next, grate 125g of dark chocolate into another bowl.

**4.** Next you need to melt the soap base, use the double boiler method as you did in the first project.

**5.** Add in your cocoa powder and essential oil to the melted soap mix. We recommend using 10 drops of cocoa oil in the mix. Once added, make sure you stir well until all ingredients are fully melted in the mixture.

**6.** Next take your bowl off the heat and transfer the mix into a heatproof glass jug. Be careful when pouring as the bowl and mixture will be very hot.

**7.** Now pour the melted soap mixture into your lined loaf tin. Remember to have your alcohol spray to hand and give the loaf a good spritz after pouring to remove any bubbles on top. Always do this quickly before the soap begins to set.

**8.** Sprinkle part of your grated chocolate on top of the warm mix. Keep some of the chocolate back for when the soap is fully cooled.

**9.** Leave your soap to cool (or until it is lukewarm) and then you can add the remaining grated chocolate on top of the soap to decorate.

**10.** Leave to fully set overnight, then remove the soap from the loaf tin mould and cut into half inch slices, we suggest carefully cutting with a wire cutter or loaf soap cutter.

**MAKES
6**

**15 MINS
TO MAKE**

# FLORAL

# FLORAL

A very simple yet effective recipe to create the perfect gift. The below recipe can be adjusted with different oils and colourants to achieve your ideal soap. Finish off with dried flowers to make it even more personal.

## YOU WILL NEED

- Heatproof bowl
- Heatproof jug
- Saucepan
- Wooden spoon
- Measuring scales
- Rubbing alcohol spray
- Thermometer (optional)

## INGREDIENTS

- 455g shea butter melt and pour base
- 6 cavity rectangular silicone mould
- Dried flowers for decoration
- Pink soap dye / colourant
- Rose essential oil

# METHOD

**1.** Set up your work surface and prepare your melt and pour soap base. Cut the 455g of soap base into small cube-size pieces, Also prepare your mould by spraying it with alcohol spray.

**2.** Prepare your dried flowers in a bowl. You can use any dried flowers for this part, but we chose to use dried gomphrena buds, peony and jasmine buds. First we pick some petals from the gomphrena and then mixed these with the peony and jasmine. Add more or less of each flower into your mix as desired. Then we recommend keeping 10-15 full gomphrema buds to one side.

**3.** Next you need to melt the soap base, use the double boiler method as you did in the first project.

**4.** Once the soap has melted, you can add in your essential oil and a little of the pink soap dye or colourant. We recommend using 10 drops of rose essential oil to the mix and keep adding more pink dye until you achieve your desired colour. Once added, make sure you stir well until fully mixed into the melted mixture.

**5.** Next take off the heat and transfer the mix into a heatproof glass jug. Be careful when pouring as the bowl and mixture will be very hot.

**6.** It's now time to pour the mixture into your mould. Slowly pour into each cavity (making sure you distribute evenly). Remember to have your alcohol spray to hand and give each bar a good spritz after pouring to remove any bubbles on top. Always do this quickly before the soaps begin to set.

**7.** Once the soaps begins to set, sprinkle your dried flowers on top in an even or random pattern (this is down to your preference). Then quickly before it fully sets, place your gomphrena buds into each soap - add one or two to each soap.

**8.** Leave your soaps to fully cool. Once set you can remove from the moulds. What beautiful soaps these make! Next time you can try this recipe with different colours and dried flowers, to create something trully unique!

## TIP

Try this recipe with different colours and dried flowers, to create your own bespoke soap designs!

MAKES
6

15 MINS
TO MAKE

# GRAPEFRUIT
# & PINK SALT

# GRAPEFRUIT & PINK SALT

Grapefruit and pink himalayan salt is a beautiful combination in soap. The grapefruit boasts sharp, sweet and uplifting scents and the pink salt acts as a natural exfoliator. This zesty soap is the ideal gift and perfect for a spa like bath experience.

## YOU WILL NEED

- Heatproof bowl
- Heatproof jug
- Saucepan
- Wooden spoon
- Measuring scales
- Rubbing alcohol spray
- Thermometer (optional)

## INGREDIENTS

- 455g shea butter melt and pour base
- 6 cavity oval mould
- 95g pink himalayan salt
- Grapefruit essential oil

# METHOD

**1.** Set up your work surface and prepare your melt and pour soap base. Do this by weighing 455g of the base. You then need to cut the 455g of soap base into smaller pieces, this will help it to melt quicker.

**2.** Next prepare your mould by spraying it with alcohol spray. Then evenly add your pink salt to the bottom of each of the six cavities in the mould.

**3.** Next you need to melt the soap base, use the double boiler method as you did in the first project.

**4.** Once the soap is melted, add in your grapefruit essential oil. We recommend using around 10 drops of grapefruit oil to the mix. The grapefruit aroma is irresistibly zesty and refreshing so just add a little more if you want it stronger. Once added, make sure you stir well until all ingredients are fully mixed into the melted soap.

**5.** Next take your bowl off the heat and transfer the mix into a heatproof glass jug. Be careful when pouring as the bowl and mixture will be very hot.

**6.** It's now time to pour the mixture into your mould. Slowly pour into each cavity (making sure you distribute evenly). Remember to have your alcohol spray to hand and give each bar a good spritz after pouring to remove any bubbles on top. Always do this quickly before the soap begins to set.

**7.** The pink salt may rise to the top of the soap, so if you want it evenly distributed, it is best to stir your soaps once they has been poured into the mould. A nice finishing touch, when they are nearly set, is to sprinkle a little extra salt on the top of each soap for decoration.

**8.** Leave your soaps to set, following the same process from the first project.

**9.** When fully set, remove each soap from it's mould. You can use straight away or store with some cling film ready to use later!

## TIP

This recipe works well in other shape moulds too! Why not try it in a square or heart shape soap mould too!

**MAKES
3**

**15 MINS
TO MAKE**

# ROSEMARY

# ROSEMARY

As well as a wonderful herb smell, rosemary soap looks natural and rustic. It makes a lovely gift when wrapped in twine with a fresh sprig of rosemary. You can also add a small slice of parchment paper for the ultimate finished look.

## YOU WILL NEED
· Heatproof bowl
· Heatproof jug
· Saucepan
· Wooden spoon
· Measuring scales
· Rubbing alcohol spray
· Thermometer (optional)

## INGREDIENTS
· 230g shea butter melt and pour base
· 3 tbsp dried rosemary
· Rosemary essential oil
· Green soap dye / colourant
· Silicone mould of choice (must include at least 3 cavities)
· Fresh rosemary, twine and parchment paper for decorating

# METHOD

**1.** Set up your work surface and prepare your melt and pour soap base. Cut the 230g of soap base into small cube-size pieces, Also prepare your chosen mould by spraying it with alcohol spray.

**2.** Cut up your dried rosemary into finely chopped pieces and sprinkle ino the bottom of your mould.

**3.** Next you need to melt the soap base, use the double boiler method as you did in the first project.

**4.** Once the soap has melted, you can add in around 10 drops of rosemary essential oil and a little of the green soap dye or colourant. Just keep adding a little more green dye until you achieve your desired colour. Make sure you stir the mixture well and keep mixing until it is fully melted.

**5.** Next take off the heat and transfer the mix into a heatproof glass jug. Be careful when pouring as the bowl and mixture will be very hot.

**6.** It's now time to pour the mixture into your mould. Slowly pour the soap into three of the cavities in your choosen mould (making sure you distribute the mix evenly). Remember to have your alcohol spray to hand and give each bar a good spritz after pouring to remove any bubbles on top. Always do this quickly before the soaps begin to set.

**7.** The rosemary will start to float to the top of the soaps. This is the desired look we want to create. However if you prefer, you can stir the dried rosemary again to make it spread through the whole soap mixture.

**8.** Leave your soaps to fully cool. Once set you can remove from the moulds.

**9.** These wonderful green soaps, never fail to disappoint! If you are making them into gifts then simply wrap with a strip of parchment paper, twine and add a sprig of fresh rosemary to finish.

**TIP**

For a lovely gift, tie a sprig of rosemary to your soap bars with twine or string.

MAKES
12

30 MINS
TO MAKE

# MINT &
# POPPY SEED

# MINT & POPPY SEED

The naturally exfoliating poppyseeds, paired with fresh zingy mint makes this the ultimate invigorating soap. Vibrant and bright, the colours make this a one of a kind.

## YOU WILL NEED

- Heatproof bowl
- Heatproof jug
- Saucepan
- Wooden spoon
- Measuring scales
- Rubbing alcohol spray
- Thermometer (optional)
- Wire soap cutter

## INGREDIENTS

- 1kg Shea Butter pour and melt base
- Blue soap dye
- 30g poppyseeds
- 2lb loaf tin (lined with cling film)

# METHOD

**1.** Set up your work surface close to your heating appliance, as you did in the first project. Prepare your loaf tin by lining with cling film and spraying inside with alcohol spray.

**2.** Weigh out 1kg of your melt and pour base. You then need to cut it into smaller pieces, this will help it to melt quicker.

**3.** To melt the soap base, use the double boiler method as you did in the first project.

**4.** Once the soap mix has melted, add the peppermint essential oil and a few drops of your soap dye or colourant to the soap base and stir well. Continue adding drops of dye until you're happy with the colour.

**5.** When the soap has reached the correct temperature or is fully melted, remove from the heat and place on a heat resistant mat or heatproof work surface. CAUTION: The bowl will be very hot so handle carefully using a tea towel or oven gloves. To get better pouring control, carefully transfer the mix into a heatproof glass jug.

**6.** It's now time to pour the mixture into your lined tin mould. Remember to give the soap a good spritz with alcohol spray.

**7.** Pour around 1/3 of your poppy seeds into the mix or until you're happy with the appearance. Stir your poppy seeds throughout the mix to get an even distribution. Make sure to move quickly so your soap base doesn't start to solidify.

**8.** Next, take your remaining poppyseeds and sprinkle them in a line down the middle of the loaf tin. You want this to be approximately half an inch wide. Add more if you want a thicker line through the soap.

**9.** Leave your soap to set in a cool dry place overnight. Due to the size of the loaf, it may take longer to set. Once set remove the soap from the mould and use a wire soap cutter to cut the loaf into slices, you want them between half an inch to one inch thick.